Russia

DEB MARSHALL

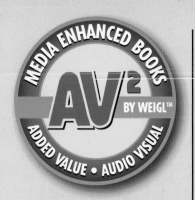

AV² provides enriched content that supplements and complements this book. Weigl's AV² books strive to create inspired learning and engage young minds in a total learning experience.

Your AV² Media Enhanced books come alive with...

Audio
Listen to sections of the book read aloud.

Key Words
Study vocabulary, and complete a matching word activity.

Video
Watch informative video clips.

Quizzes
Test your knowledge.

Embedded Weblinks
Gain additional information for research.

Slide Show
View images and captions, and prepare a presentation.

Go to www.av2books.com, and enter this book's unique code.

BOOK CODE

Q 4 8 5 3 2 8

AV² by Weigl brings you media enhanced books that support active learning.

Try This!
Complete activities and hands-on experiments.

... and much, much more!

Published by AV² by Weigl
350 5th Avenue, 59th Floor
New York, NY 10118
Website: www.av2books.com   www.weigl.com

Library of Congress Cataloging-in-Publication Data

Marshall, Deb, 1959-
 Russia / Deb Marshall.
   pages ; cm. -- (Exploring countries)
Audience: Grade 5 to 8.
ISBN 978-1-62127-254-0 (hardcover : alk. paper) -- ISBN 978-1-62127-260-1 (softcover : alk. paper)
1. Russia--Juvenile literature. 2. Russia--Description and travel--Juvenile literature. I. Title. II. Series: Exploring countries (AV2 by Weigl)
DK29.2.M37 2013
947--dc23
                        2012041280

Printed in the United States of America in North Mankato, Minnesota
1 2 3 4 5 6 7 8 9 17 16 15 14 13

052013
WEP040413

Project Coordinator Heather Kissock
Art Director Terry Paulhus

Photo Credits
Every reasonable effort has been made to trace ownership and to obtain permission to reprint copyright material. The publishers would be pleased to have any errors or omissions brought to their attention so that they may be corrected in subsequent printings.

Weigl acknowledges Getty Images as its primary image supplier for this title.

Contents

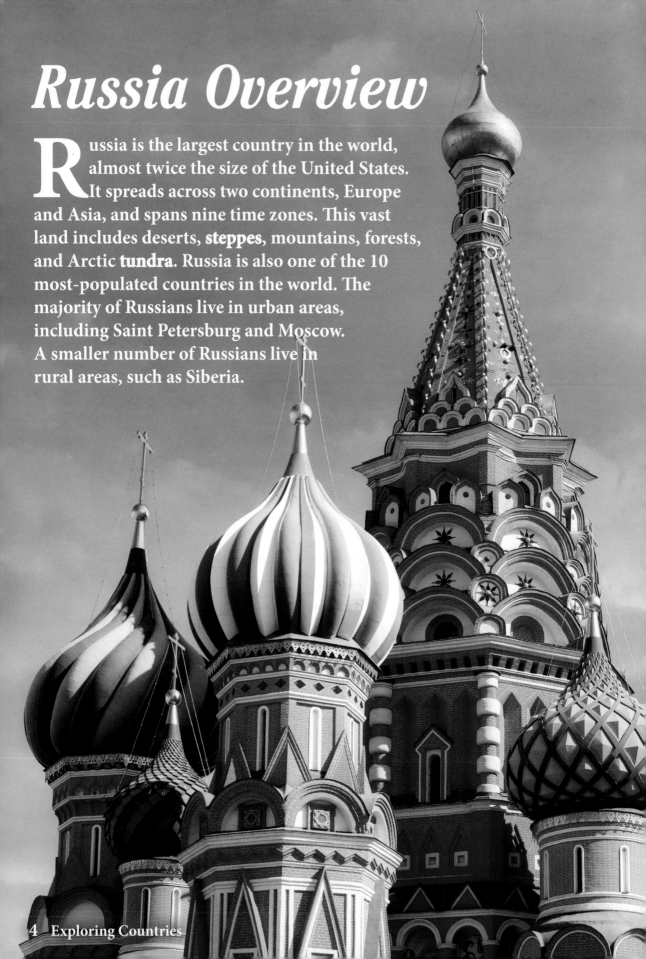

Russia Overview

Russia is the largest country in the world, almost twice the size of the United States. It spreads across two continents, Europe and Asia, and spans nine time zones. This vast land includes deserts, **steppes**, mountains, forests, and Arctic **tundra**. Russia is also one of the 10 most-populated countries in the world. The majority of Russians live in urban areas, including Saint Petersburg and Moscow. A smaller number of Russians live in rural areas, such as Siberia.

Though Siberia makes up three-fourths of Russia's land, only 20 percent of the population lives there. Vast forested areas cover the region.

In Moscow, Russia's largest city, the huge GUM indoor mall attracts both residents and visitors.

Folk dance companies perform across the country. They reflect the dance traditions of Russia's different cultural groups.

Puppet theaters in Moscow and other cities are a popular form of entertainment for children in Russia.

The brown bear has long been a symbol of Russia. Brown bears living in Russia are larger than the bears found in other areas of Europe.

Exploring Russia

The Russian Federation, as the country is officially called, covers 6.6 million square miles (17.1 million square kilometers). It has the longest border in the world. Fourteen countries line this border, which is 12,580 miles (20,240 km) long. The Ural Mountains divide Russia into eastern and western parts. Forested areas cover almost half the country.

Finland

Estonia

Latvia

Belarus

Moscow

Moscow

Ukraine

Mount Elbrus

Georgia

Kazakstan

Map Legend

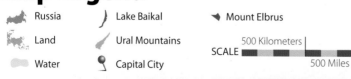

Russia	Lake Baikal	Mount Elbrus
Land	Ural Mountains	500 Kilometers
Water	Capital City	SCALE 500 Miles

Mount Elbrus

At 18,510 feet (5,642 meters), Mount Elbrus is the highest mountain in Russia. A **dormant** volcano, it is part of the Caucasus mountain range.

Ural Mountains

RUSSIA

Lake Baikal

N

Mongolia

China

North
Korea

Japan

Moscow

Moscow is the capital of Russia. The city contains historic churches, museums, and palaces. Many of them are in the walled area called the Kremlin in the center of the city.

Ural Mountains

At 250 million years old, the Urals are the oldest mountains in the world. This mountain range is more than 1,500 miles (2,400 km) long. It forms the traditional boundary between Europe and Asia.

Lake Baikal

Lake Baikal in Siberia has the most water of any lake on Earth. It contains one-fifth of the world's freshwater. It is also the deepest lake in the world.

LAND AND CLIMATE

R ussia stretches 5,000 miles (8,050 km) west to east, from the Gulf of Finland to the Bering Strait. Scientists divide the country into four climate and soil zones. These are the tundra, the forest, the steppes, and the mountainous zones.

One-tenth of Russia's land area is tundra. In much of this northern area, the surface soil is frozen for most of the year. During the summer, the top 3 to 10 inches (7.5 to 25 centimeters) of soil thaws. Even then, the land below the surface may be frozen to a depth of nearly 2,000 feet (610 m). So little rain or snow falls in Russia's Arctic tundra that some of the area is considered a desert. Shrubs, dwarf trees, and moss are the only plants able to survive the harsh environment. South of the tundra lies an area called the **taiga**, with vast areas of evergreen forests. South of the forests, the grassy plains called the steppes stretch across Russia.

The taiga covers most of Siberia in north-central Russia.

Mountains along the southern border prevent warm winds from the south from entering Russia. These mountains include the Caucasus range, which runs east-west from the Caspian Sea to the Black Sea. Most of the country's coastal waters, lakes, and rivers freeze for a large part of the year. Russia's main cropland, in the southwestern part of the country, has a short growing season, and rain is scarce.

Winters in Russia are long and harsh. Summers are short and cool. The country has recorded the world's lowest temperature outside Antarctica. In 1892, Verkhoyansk in Siberia had a temperature of −90° Fahrenheit (−69° Celsius). About half of Russia has **permafrost** beneath the surface. In the Moscow region, snow covers the ground for about five months each year. Farther north, snow remains for eight to nine months.

Two mountain ranges lie along the Kamchatka Peninsula in far eastern Russia. Most of the land is tundra.

PLANTS AND ANIMALS

The plants of Russia are as varied as its regions. Lichens, mosses, and shrubs grow in the tundra. Trees such as cedar, fir, pine, and spruce thrive in the taiga. A variety of grasses flourish on the steppes. The buttercup flower is found all over Russia. It can survive extremely cold temperatures. A variety of trees grow in southern Russia, including **conifers**, aspen, birch, elm, maple, spruce, oak, and hornbeam. The hornbeam tree is small, with a twisted trunk and short branches. Russia has more forested land than any other country. It is known as the "lungs of Europe" because its trees add so much oxygen to the air.

The animal life of Russia also varies from region to region. Animals that roam the tundra include polar bears, muskoxen, lemmings, snowy owls, and reindeer. In the forests, squirrels, martens, elk, foxes, muskrats, and bears search for food. Siberian tigers live in the birch forests of Russia's Far East. Snow leopards and **pikas** can be found in mountainous areas in the Asian part of Russia. The musk deer, which lives in Siberia's taiga forests, has a face that looks like a kangaroo's. Male deer have two long teeth, similar to tusks.

Fewer than 500 Siberian tigers survive in nature. The Russian government has made it illegal to hunt the tigers, and their numbers are increasing.

Plants and Animals BY THE NUMBERS

10 feet
Length of the largest cat in the world, the Siberian tiger, from head to tail. (3 m)

5 to 6.5 feet
Wingspan of the Eurasian eagle owls of Russia , the largest owls in the world. (1.5 to 2 m)

2,000
Number of **species** of plants and animals that live in and around Lake Baikal. The majority of these species cannot be found anywhere else in the world.

NATURAL RESOURCES

Russia's petroleum and natural gas deposits are some of the largest in the world. They are found mostly in western Siberia and the Ural Mountains. Pipelines carry oil and gas across the vast country. Some of it is exported to other countries around the world. Russia also has large deposits of diamonds, copper, lead, and zinc, as well as one-sixth of the world's iron ore.

This huge nation is one of the largest producers of coal, most of which is mined in the Kuznetsk Basin in western Siberia. The country generates two-thirds of its electricity by burning coal, natural gas, or oil. It also uses **hydroelectric** power plants to produce electricity.

Fish in Russia's coastal waters, rivers, and lakes are an important food source. In the northern Barents Sea and the White Sea, fishers catch blue whiting, cod, haddock, and herring. Pollock and salmon are caught in the Pacific Ocean. Some species of fish are protected in large reserves, including the Atlantic Salmon Reserve.

Russia is a leading producer of grain. On the steppes, an area called the Black Earth Belt is known for its rich, dark soil. Here, farmers grow many different crops, including barley, oats, and wheat. They also produce potatoes and sugar beets.

More than 90 percent of the potatoes grown in Russia are raised in family gardens and on small farms.

Natural Resources BY THE NUMBERS

40% Portion of the world's natural gas that is found in Russia.

725 billion tons
Amount of coal estimated to be in the Kuznetsk Basin region. (660 billion tonnes)

1/5
Fraction of the world's timber growing in the forests of Siberia.

TOURISM

Ancient cities, varied cultures, and vast landscapes all draw tourists to Russia. Moscow and Saint Petersburg are popular destinations for visitors. In Moscow, the 250-acre (100-hectare) Kremlin contains Russian government offices along with museums and churches that are hundreds of years old. The oldest of these is the Cathedral of the Annunciation, which was completed in 1479.

Onion-shaped domes top many old churches throughout Russia.

Saint Petersburg offers visitors a mix of Western European and Russian architecture. Much of the city was built in the early 1700s, when Emperor Peter the Great ruled Russia. He planned to create a beautiful and impressive new city. Today, Saint Petersburg has many museums, theaters, and churches. One of the largest museums in the world, the Hermitage, was once the private art museum of Empress Catherine the Great. Its paintings include Western European works, as well as Asian art.

The Hermitage has about 3 million items in its collection.

The Golden Ring of Ancient Cities is a group of towns near Moscow. Russia has preserved them as living museums. One of the oldest of these cities, Suzdal, dates back to 1024. With its white walls and bell towers, it contains some of Russia's best historical architecture.

A destination that was almost unknown until 1941 is now a popular tourist attraction. The Valley of the Geysers is the second-largest geyser field in the world. It is found on the Kamchatka Peninsula.

Cruises on the Volga River are also popular. The Volga is Europe's longest river and one of Russia's main waterways. Cruises can be taken from Moscow to Saint Petersburg and to the Golden Ring of Ancient Cities. The Trans-Siberian Railroad takes tourists across Russia from Moscow, through Siberia, and all the way to the city of Vladivostok on Russia's east coast.

The Trans-Siberian Railroad curves around the southern shore of Lake Baikal for part of its length.

INDUSTRY

8,000 square miles Amount of land in which trees are cut down for lumber every year. (20,000 sq. km)

1/6 Portion of Russia's land that is used for agriculture.

10.3 million Barrels Amount of oil produced per day in Russia.

From 1922 to 1991, Russia and 14 other countries were part of the Union of Soviet Socialist Republics (USSR), or Soviet Union. The USSR was a **communist** country, and the government controlled all industries. After the breakup of the Soviet Union during the 1990s, individuals in Russia began to own and control many businesses. However, the government of the new Russian Federation continues to control energy production, which is one of the country's most important industries.

Russia is a world leader in oil production. It is also a major producer of many other minerals. The country's exports of oil, natural gas, metals, and timber account for more than 80 percent of all the goods and services Russia sends to other countries.

Minerals mined in Russia are used in the country's manufacturing industry. Russia's factories produce metals, machinery, cement, chemicals, motor vehicles, and other goods. They also manufacture trains and agricultural equipment, as well as advanced aircraft and aerospace products. In the early 21st century, making food and beverage products became an important industry. The production of cell phones and personal computers also grew.

Nearly 3 million cars are sold in Russia every year. The size of this market has led many foreign companies to manufacture cars in the country.

GOODS AND SERVICES

Russia's leading imports from other countries include machinery and transportation equipment, food, and chemicals. The country's primary trading partners are China, Germany, Ukraine, the Netherlands, Italy, and Poland. Trading partners are nations to which a country sends exports or from which it receives imports.

One of Russia's most famous, and expensive, exports is **caviar**. Many people think that **sturgeon** from the Caspian Sea, located largely in Russia, produce the world's best caviar. In recent years, however, overfishing, **poaching**, and loss of habitat have greatly reduced the number of Caspian Sea sturgeon. Some scientists believe this fish is in danger of dying out completely.

Today, many Russians are employed in service industries. Workers in these industries provide a service to other people, rather than producing goods. Service industry workers include store clerks, restaurant employees, plumbers, bus and train drivers, teachers, and doctors.

Russia's cities have modern public transportation systems. However, people still use horses and buggies in parts of rural Russia. Cell phones are widely used in urban areas, but large areas of the country where few people live have little or no cell phone service.

60%
Portion of all Russian workers employed in service industries.

256 MILLION
Number of cell phones owned by Russians.

10th **in the World**
Russia's rank compared to other countries for number of Internet users.

Powered by overhead electrical lines, trolleys carry passengers throughout Moscow.

INDIGENOUS PEOPLES

The largest group of **indigenous** people in Siberia is the Buryat. They are a **Mongol** people. Their land became part of Russia in 1689. By tradition, they are **nomadic** herders who raise cattle, horses, sheep, and goats. Today, their customs and traditions are mixed with Russian culture.

Since the 10th century, the Tatars have lived in the forests and steppes of Siberia, as well as along the Volga River in west-central Russia. Many Tatars now live in cities and work in various industries. Some, however, still make their living by farming and herding cattle and sheep.

The Evenk people, also sometimes called the Evenki, have traditionally lived in northern Siberia. Some survived mainly by hunting. Others herded reindeer. Under the government of the Soviet Union, in the 20th century, many Evenk were forced to become farmers.

Indigenous Peoples BY THE NUMBERS

ABOUT 550,000
Number of Buryat living in Russia today.

3.8%
Portion of the Russian population who are Tatars.

35,000
About how many Evenk people live in Russia.

Traditional Tatar dress for men and women consists of a long shirt and pants. Fancy stitching decorates women's clothes.

THE AGE OF EXPLORATION

The first Russian kingdom was set up in the 9th century by the Rus people. It included part of today's European Russia. Over time, Russians moved eastward, to gain more land and to hunt fur-bearing animals. By the late 1500s, Russia controlled most of Siberia. Russia's territory extended to the Pacific Ocean by 1640.

Russians began exploring the Pacific Coast of North America in 1648. Semen I. Dezhnev led the first expedition. He may have been the first European to learn that water separates North America from the eastern tip of Russia. The Great Northern Expedition lasted from 1733 to 1743. Russian ships explored and mapped thousands of miles (km) of the Arctic and Pacific coasts. In 1741, a Russian expedition led by Danish navigator Vitus Bering explored the Aleutian Islands and the southern coast of Alaska.

Russian settlements were set up along the Pacific Coast of North America in the late 1700s, extending as far south as California. The Russians hunted fur-bearing animals, such as seals, or traded with native peoples for furs. By the mid-1800s, the money that could be made from fur trading declined. As a result, so did Russia's interest in North America. The United States purchased Alaska from Russia in 1867.

$7.2 million
Amount the United States paid to buy Alaska from Russia.

3,482
Number of Russian coins, dated to 1619, discovered on Faddeya Island in the Arctic. The coins are believed to be the remains of a shipwrecked Russian expedition from about 1640.

1784 Year that Russian fur traders settled on Kodiak Island in what is now Alaska.

In 1741, Vitus Bering's ship was wrecked on an island near Kamchatka. Bering died on the island.

EARLY SETTLERS

People have lived in what is now Russia since 2000 BC. One of the earliest invaders were the Cimmerians. They were a Slavic tribe that lived north of the Black Sea in southeastern Europe around 1200 BC. They may have originally come from Iran.

The Scythians were a nomadic people who often traveled on horseback. Pictures of horses are common in Scythian rugs and other decorated objects.

By 700 BC, the Scythians had invaded from Asia. These people ruled what is now southern Russia until 200 BC, when the Sarmatians from Central Asia invaded. All these early tribes hunted, fished, and farmed. Tribes that lived on the steppes also raised cattle.

The Goths were a Germanic tribe who came to Russia in about 200 AD. They defeated the Sarmatians. The Goths ruled the area until 370, when the Huns, warrior tribes from Asia, conquered them.

Vikings from northern Europe also settled in Russia. Scientists have found evidence of Viking settlements dating back to as early as 750. Viking leader Rurik founded the city of Novgorod in 862. He began the Rurik Dynasty, which ruled Russia until the 16th century.

Scythian artists were highly skilled at working with gold. They created beautiful necklaces and other types of jewelry.

From 770 to 830, merchants, explorers, and traders also came to Russia from the area around the Baltic Sea in eastern Europe. They were searching for amber, wax, honey, furs, and timber. Later, traders from northern Iran and Africa came looking for the same materials, as well as slaves.

In about the middle of the 9th century, the Rus people came to Russia. The Rus may have been traders from Scandinavia, in northern Europe, or Slavs from eastern Europe. They settled along the northern part of the Volga River. The Rus established the first state of modern Russia and called it Kievan Rus. They had adopted the Christian religion and brought it to Russia.

In 1238, Mongols from eastern Asia invaded Russia and conquered Kievan Rus. Fleeing the Mongols, many people moved to the area around present-day Moscow. The city grew from a small trading post to a large town.

Mongol control gradually grew weaker. It lasted until 1480, when Russian prince Ivan III refused to pay taxes to the Mongols. A new state called Muscovy arose, and Ivan was crowned the first **tsar** of Muscovy. During his rule, Ivan acquired more land for Muscovy. The rulers who followed him extended their control over larger and larger areas.

Early Settlers BY THE NUMBERS

438

Year that Derbent, the oldest surviving city in Russia, was founded. The city is well-known for its ancient cemeteries.

1547–1584

Years Ivan the Terrible ruled as tsar of Russia.

1721

Year Peter the Great became the first Russian tsar to use the title *emperor*.

Ivan III's grandson, Ivan IV, was the first ruler to be crowned tsar of Russia. He became known as Ivan the Terrible because of his cruelty.

POPULATION

Russia has a population of more than 142 million. Most people live in the European part of Russia, west of the Ural Mountains. Almost 75 percent of Russians live in urban areas.

Since the breakup of the Soviet Union, Russia has experienced a decline in population. Many people are choosing to have small families, and **life expectancy** has dropped for several reasons. These include high rates of smoking, abuse of alcohol, pollution, poor **nutrition**, and lack of health care. Men's life expectancy has dropped more than women's.

Under communism, health care was free. The Russian government still tries to provide health care for its citizens. However, medicines and equipment are sometimes in short supply.

The population drop has been slowed somewhat by **immigration**. Ethnic Russians from countries that used to be part of the Soviet Union are moving to Russia. The term *ethnic Russians* refers to people who are descended from the ancient Rus.

More than 10 million people live in Moscow, and many Russians have moved there from other parts of the country. New skyscrapers house businesses that draw job seekers.

POLITICS AND GOVERNMENT

After the Soviet Union came to an end, Russia's government changed from a communist system with one political party to a democratic system with many political parties. By choosing from the candidates of these parties, Russians elect a president. He or she serves a six-year term and is limited to two **consecutive** terms. The president appoints a prime minister to be the head of the Council of Ministers. The council includes leaders of governmental departments and other people appointed by the president. This is the executive branch of government.

The Federal Assembly is the legislative branch of government. It is made up of two parts, the State Duma and the Federation Council. Half of the members of the Federation Council are appointed by local governors and half by local legislatures. Members of the Duma are elected. The Duma makes the country's laws. Legislation passed by the Duma must be approved by the Federation Council and the president before becoming law. However, the Duma can override disapproval by the Federation Council and send legislation directly to the president.

The highest body in Russia's judicial branch is the Supreme Court. It oversees all other courts in the country. It is also the final **court of appeal**. A **constitutional** court reviews all of Russia's laws and treaties.

The State Duma building in Moscow where the legislature meets was constructed in the 1930s.

CULTURAL GROUPS

The cultural heritage of Russia includes the influences of the early Slavs. The Mongols brought their Asian culture in the early 1200s. Into this is mixed the cultural influences of Western Europe. Peter the Great and rulers who followed him admired Western European arts and customs and brought them to Russia.

The Russian language uses the Cyrillic alphabet, which has 32 letters.

The largest cultural group in the country is Russians, who make up 80 percent of the population. They trace their culture back to the Slavs. Russian is the country's official language.

The next-largest groups are the Tatars and Ukrainians. Most Tatars are Muslim. They make up about half the population of Tatarstan, a republic in eastern Russia. Almost 2 million Ukrainians live in Russia today. Ukraine was once part of the Soviet Union, and many Russians moved to Ukraine. Many Ukrainians also moved to Russia, and some still speak their native language in addition to Russian.

Nesting dolls are a traditional Russian toy. They are often painted in bright colors.

During the years of the Soviet Union, the government favored ethnic Russians. It forced people who were not ethnic Russians from their traditional lands. The land was then used for government-run farms and factories. The government made people of other backgrounds learn Russian. It also tried to stop them from speaking their native languages. Since the end of the Soviet era, many cultural groups have demanded more independence. They want to have more control over their traditional area of the country and its resources. More children are learning both Russian and the language of their **ancestors**.

The Soviet government also discouraged people from practicing their religion. As a result, many Russians do not follow a religion today. About one-sixth of the population practices Russian Orthodoxy, a form of Christianity. Muslims are the second-largest religious group. There are small numbers of practicing Protestants, Jews, and Buddhists.

The Soviet government destroyed many Russian Orthodox churches. Since the end of the Soviet era, more people are following this religion.

Cultural Groups BY THE NUMBERS

10–15%
Portion of the population that is Muslim.

120 Number of cultural groups, besides Russians, in the country.

100 Number of different languages spoken, in addition to Russian.

ARTS AND ENTERTAINMENT

In the 1800s and early 1900s, Russian composers and writers created many works of classical music, drama, and literature that are still performed and read today. Orchestras around the world play the music of 19th-century composer Peter Ilich Tchaikovsky. His music is used in the ballets *Swan Lake* and *The Nutcracker*.

In the early 1900s, the Russian jeweler Peter Carl Fabergé made decorative objects shaped like eggs. Inside each "egg" was a small surprise.

Russian ballet became well known around the world starting in the mid-1800s. Several leading ballet companies still perform today. They include the Bolshoi Ballet of Moscow and the Mariinsky Ballet of Saint Petersburg, which used to be called the Imperial Russian Ballet and later the Kirov Ballet.

The Bolshoi Ballet often performs the ballet *Sleeping Beauty*, which uses music composed by Tchaikovsky.

Peter Carl Fabergé's decorative eggs were made with gold, silver, and gemstones found in Russia. In the late 19th and early 20th centuries, he was jeweler and goldsmith to the royal family of Russia. Many of the 50 eggs he made for the family can now be seen in museums.

The Pushkin Museum of Fine Arts in Moscow holds works of Western European art. Also in Moscow, the Obraztsov Puppet Theater is the largest puppet theater in Russia. Children can learn about Russian folklore through puppet plays. South of Moscow is the estate of Leo Tolstoy, which is now a museum. Tolstoy wrote what many experts think are two of the Western world's finest novels, *War and Peace* and *Anna Karenina*.

Chess is a popular pastime. Tournaments are held all over the country. Russian players have won many of the international tournaments that determine the world champion.

People can visit Tolstoy's house and lands in Yasnaya Polyana in central Russia. He wrote many of his novels there.

More Than 200
Number of museums in Saint Petersburg.

50 Million
Number of chess players in Russia, according to a 2012 survey.

$18.5 million
Highest price paid by a collector for a Fabergé egg.

SPORTS

Russia is a world leader when it comes to sports. Russian athletes rank highly in most Olympic events. At the 2012 Summer Olympics, held in London, United Kingdom, Russia placed third among all countries taking part in total number of medals won. Russian athletes won gold medals in boxing, judo, wrestling, swimming, high jump, and rhythmic gymnastics, among other events. Russia finished fourth in total number of gold medals won.

Sports in Russia are governed by the Ministry of Sport of the Russian Federation. It is also called Minisport. The ministry is responsible for planning and applying the government's policies on physical fitness and sport. The government promotes athletic activities, especially team sports. Russia has many athletic clubs, stadiums, recreation centers, and other sports facilities. Both children and adults participate in sports camps and clubs.

In the sport of bandy, the sticks must be a different color from the ball.

The Russian men's volleyball team won a gold medal in the 2012 London Olympics.

Russia created sport schools when it was part of the Soviet Union. Children as young as five years old were sent to these **boarding schools** to specialize in a sport. Today, 3.5 million Russian children still attend these schools. They are no longer boarding schools, and children are not expected to start their sport at such young ages.

A popular winter sport called bandy is played on ice. It is similar in some ways to ice hockey, but players use their sticks to get a ball, not a puck, into the goal. There are 11 players and a goalkeeper on each team. Many people watch from the sidelines. Another favorite sport on ice is figure skating. National championships are held each year.

More people in Russia play or watch soccer than any other sport. Many Russians also enjoy gymnastics, basketball, and skiing. Tennis is growing in popularity. One of the top-ranked women's tennis players in the world is Russia's Maria Sharapova. She started playing professionally in 2001. In 2012, she won a silver medal in the Olympics. Russian players also won a bronze medal in women's doubles tennis.

Sports
BY THE NUMBERS

2014 — Year the Russian city of Sochi hosts the Winter Olympics.

82 and 24 — Total medals and gold medals won by Russian athletes at the 2012 Summer Olympics.

2018 — Year that the soccer men's World Cup tournament will be held in Russia.

18,000 — Number of people who took part in the 2013 Moscow Ski Track, an annual cross-country ski race.

Maria Sharapova won the women's singles title at the 2012 French Open tennis tournament.

Mapping Russia

We use many tools to interpret maps and to understand the locations of features such as cities, states, lakes, and rivers. The map below has many tools to help interpret information on the map of Russia.

Map of Russia

MAP LEGEND

★ Capital City   /\ River   \ Longitude & Latitude

● City   -·-·- Country Border   ▢ Russia

🗺 Body of Water   ▢ Other Countries

N W E S

SCALE
0   750 km
0   750 mi

Mapping Tools

- The compass rose shows north, south, east, and west. The points in between represent northeast, northwest, southeast, and southwest.
- The map scale shows that the distances on a map represent much longer distances in real life. If you measure the distance between objects on a map, you can use the map scale to calculate the actual distance in miles or kilometers between those two points.

- The lines of latitude and longitude are long lines that appear on maps. The lines of latitude run east to west and measure how far north or south of the equator a place is located. The lines of longitude run north to south and measure how far east or west of the Prime Meridian a place is located. A location on a map can be found by using the two numbers where latitude and longitude meet. This number is called a coordinate and is written using degrees and direction. For example, the city of Los Angeles would be found at 34°N and 118°W on a map.

Map It!

Using the map and the appropriate tools, complete the activities below.

Locating with latitude and longitude

1. What city is located at 59°N and 30°E?
2. What part of Russia is located at 60°N and 105°E?
3. What sea is found on the map using the coordinates 43°N and 34°E?

Distances between points

4. Using the map scale and a ruler, calculate the approximate distance between the cities of Saint Petersburg and Moscow.
5. Using the map scale and a ruler, calculate the approximate distance between Murmansk and Volgograd.
6. Using the map scale and a ruler, find the approximate length of Lake Baikal.

Quiz Time

Test your knowledge of Russia by answering these questions.

1 What country was Russia part of before it became a federation in 1991?

2 What is the name of the deepest lake in Russia and in the world?

3 How many countries border Russia?

4 In what city is the Hermitage art museum found?

5 Who led the Russian expedition that explored Alaska in 1741?

6 What is the most popular spectator and participant sport in Russia?

7 What was Peter Carl Fabergé famous for making?

8 What mountain range forms the boundary between Europe and Asia?

9 What area did Russia sell to the United States in 1867?

10 Who was the country of Russia named after?

ANSWERS

1. The Union of Soviet Socialist Republics
2. Lake Baikal
3. 14
4. Saint Petersburg
5. Vitus Bering
6. Soccer
7. Jeweled eggs
8. The Ural Mountains
9. Alaska
10. The Rus people

Key Words

ancestors: people from whom an individual or group is descended
autonomous: having self-government
boarding schools: educational institutions where the students live during the school year
caviar: the salty eggs of a sturgeon or other large fish, eaten as a treat
communist: describes a system of government in which a single party controls all businesses and agriculture, all property is publicly owned, and people work and are paid according to their abilities
conifers: evergreen trees and shrubs that have cones
consecutive: following one after another in order
constitutional: having to do with a constitution, a document containing the basic laws of a nation, state, or social group

court of appeal: a high court that reviews decisions made by lower courts and may change those decisions
dormant: not active for a time
hydroelectric: producing electricity using the energy of moving water, such as in a river
immigration: moving to a new country or area to live and work
indigenous: native to a particular area
life expectancy: the amount of time, on average, that a person in a certain population group can expect to live
Mongol: a member of a group of people native to the part of Asia that includes the present-day country of Mongolia
nomadic: related to a people who move around in search of food, water, and other needs

nutrition: food substances that the body needs for good health
permafrost: ground that is always frozen
pikas: small, short-eared animals similar to rabbits
poaching: hunting or fishing illegally
reserves: areas of land or water that are set apart
species: groups of individuals with common characteristics
steppes: dry, flat areas covered with grass
sturgeon: large, long fish with thick skin covered in bony plates
taiga: a damp, northern forest where evergreen trees grow
tsar: a ruler of Russia
tundra: flat land in which soil below the surface is always frozen and only small plants can grow

Index

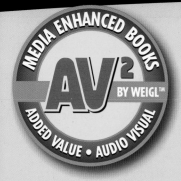

Log on to www.av2books.com

AV² by Weigl brings you media enhanced books that support active learning. Go to www.av2books.com, and enter the special code found on page 2 of this book. You will gain access to enriched and enhanced content that supplements and complements this book. Content includes video, audio, weblinks, quizzes, a slide show, and activities.

AV² Online Navigation

Book Pages
AV² pages directly correspond to pages in the book.

Audio
Listen to sections o the book read alou

Video
Watch informative video clips.

Embedded Weblinks
Gain additional information for research.

Key Words
Study vocabulary, and complete a matching word activity.

Quizzes
Test your knowledge.

Slide Show
View images and captions, and prepare a presentation.

Try This!
Complete activities and hands-on experiments.

AV² was built to bridge the gap between print and digital. We encourage you to tell us what you like and what you want to see in the future.

Sign up to be an AV² Ambassador at www.av2books.com/ambassador.